Brown As an Acorn

written by **Molly Dingles**

illustrated by **Walter Velez**

dingles & company New Jersey

For Skip & Janine

First printing

PUBLISHED BY dingles&company

P.O. Box 508 • Sea Girt, New Jersey • 08750
WEBSITE: www.dingles.com • E-MAIL: info@dingles.com

Library of Congress Catalog Card No.: 2004091475
ISBN: 1-891997-35-1

Printed in the United States of America

●

ART DIRECTED & DESIGNED BY Barbie Lambert
DESIGN ASSISTANT Erin Collity
ENGLISH EDITED BY Andrea Curley
EDUCATION CONSULTANT Kathleen P. Miller
PREPRESS BY Pixel Graphics, Inc.

Molly Dingles

is the author of *Jinka Jinka Jelly Bean* and *Little Lee Lee's Birthday Bang*. As Judy Zocchi, she has written the *Paulie & Sasha* series. She is a writer and lyricist who holds a bachelor's degree in fine arts/theater from Mount Saint Mary's College and a master's degree in educational theater from New York University. She lives in Manasquan, New Jersey, with her husband, David.

Walter Velez

was born in New York. He attended the High School of Art and Design and later the School of Visual Arts. He has done illustration work for many major book and gaming companies. He is known for the popular series *Thieves World* as well as the *Myth* series for Ace Books. He has also produced trading cards for *Goosebumps* and *Dune*. In addition, Walter has illustrated several *Star Wars* books for Random House. He lives in Queens, New York, with his wife, Kriti, and daughter, Kassandra.

The Community of Color series is more than just a series of books about colors. The series demonstrates how individual people, places, and things combine to form a community. It allows children to view the world in segments and then experience the wonderment and value of the community as a whole.

Brown as a cabin

Brown loaf of bread

Brown as a chipmunk

Brown bird to be fed.

Brown as a beaver

Brown chocolate cake

Brown as an acorn

Brown dock
in the lake.

Brown as a mud pie

Brown icy tea

Brown as a squirrel

Brown trunk of a tree.

The color Brown is all around.

ABOUT COLOR

Use the Community of Color series to teach your child to identify the most basic colors and to help him or her relate these colors to objects in the real world. ASK:

- What color is this book about?
- Can you name the brown things in this camp?
- Can you find a brown chipmunk in this picture?
- What brown dessert is in this picture?

ABOUT COMMUNITY

Use the Community of Color series to teach your child how he or she is an important part of the community. Explain to your child what a community is.

- A community is a place where people live, work, and play together.
- Your family is a community.
- Your school is a community.
- Your neighborhood is a community.
- The world is one big community.

Everyone plays an important part in making a community work - moms, dads, boys, girls, police officers, firefighters, teachers, mail carriers, garbage collectors, store clerks, and even animals are all important parts of a community. USE THESE QUESTIONS TO FURTHER THE CONVERSATION:

- How are the people at this camp interacting with one another?
- How are the people different from one another? How are they the same?
- What do they have in common?
- How is the community you see in this book like your community? How is it different?
- Describe your community.

ABOUT FEELINGS

Colors can describe as well as evoke different emotions. Encourage your child to describe the feelings that the color brown inspires.

- How does the color brown make you feel?
- Name your favorite brown thing in this book. Why is it your favorite?
- Name your favorite brown thing at home. Why is it your favorite?
- Can you tell how the people in the picture feel by looking at their faces? Do you ever feel the same way? When? Why?

TRY SOMETHING NEW... Help those in need! With your parents help, have an ice-tea stand and donate the money you earn to a charity of your choice.

community of color series